Given to Forgive

GIVEN TO FORGIVE

CHERYL STASINOWSKY

WORD SCRIBE

GIVEN TO FORGIVE
Copyright © 2014 by Cheryl Stasinowsky

All rights reserved. No part of this book may be reproduced, stored in a retrieval system, or transmitted in any form or by any means-electronic, mechanical, photocopy, recording, or otherwise-without prior written permission of the copyright owner, except by a reviewer who wishes to quote brief passages in connection with a review for inclusion in a magazine, website, newspaper, podcast, or broadcast. Cheryl Stasinowsky does not capitalize the name of satan or any reference to the devil.

All Scripture quotations, unless otherwise indicated, are taken from the New King James Version of the Bible. Copyright © 1982 by Thomas Nelson, Inc.

Interior design and cover design provided by www.truenorthpublish.com.

Published by WordScribe

ISBN: 970-0-0923066-0-4

For Worldwide Distribution. Published in the United States of America.

Dedication

*I dedicate this book to my children, their children, and to the generations that I will never have an opportunity to personally speak to.
I am writing this book with you in my heart.
I have forgiven for you, so that you can be free.
Yes, you will have your own challenges with forgiving people, but I hand you what I have learned and been given to for you. I pray that you, too, will be given to forgive those who hurt you.
I bless you on your own personal journey of forgiveness.
I love you and am praying for you right now, as I am alive.*

How awesome is that!

My Family

Table of Contents

Acknowledgements
Endorsements
Introduction

Chapter 1: Forgive or Not to Forgive 17
Chapter 2: The Power of Forgiveness 21
Chapter 3: The Power of Unforgiveness 25
Chapter 4: Our Emotions Count Too 31
Chapter 5: A Friend Named Guilt 35
Chapter 6: Influence of the Past 39
Chapter 7: Will You for Me? 43
Chapter 8: The Example of a Parent 47
Chapter 9: Generational Influences 53
Chapter 10: Those Repeat Offenders 57
Chapter 11: For a Future Time 61
Chapter 12: Don't Forget to Forgive God 63
Chapter 13: Forgive Yourself Too 67
Chapter 14: Concluding Points 71
Chapter 15: Scriptures 75

About the Author
More Titles by Cheryl Stasinowsky

Acknowledgements

Jesus, You are my example! You faced far worse while You were here on this earth, and in the last moments of Your life, while hanging in pain on the cross, You forgave those who put You there. Thank You for forgiving me and teaching me so many areas of forgiveness. I love You and will serve and trust You all the days of my life!

Mom, thank you for bringing me into this world and for loving me. We have worked through tough things over the years, but we are still standing and talking and loving each other. I love you and forgive you!

Wally, my husband of 32 years, I love you. We have given each other many opportunities to learn about forgiveness over these years, thank you! You have supported me through yet another book and have been my biggest fan. Thank you for loving me through all of these years as I was learning how to forgive...

Amber and Daniel, my daughter and new son, I love you both. Thank you for all of your love and support on yet another book. Many of these chapters you have walked out with me and experienced the freedom that is within these pages. May you continue to apply what is in this book, love, and forgive each other and others daily. It will change your future forever!!

Jordan, my son, I love you! You and I are alike in many ways, and, at times, we knock heads but we always get through it. I am proud of you and appreciate you as my son. I love how you think and see life.

Jean, you have endured yet another book with me and contributed commas, and omitting of words. You have graciously adjusted my sentences and made this book so much better. Thank you for the hours you put into this and for all the 'that' words you deleted. I appreciate you more than words can speak!

Endorsements

Cheryl Stasinowsky' new book, GIVEN to Forgive, is a must read. Her fresh, experienced insights are illuminating and life changing. Unforgiveness is a toxic bitterness which crafts mean, miser people, as Cheryl so perfectly states, hurt people hurt people. Reading this book will open to you the amazing power of forgiveness and gift you a whole life of peace, freedom, and love. We celebrate the treasures shared by the life and ministry of Cheryl Stasinowsky. GIVEN to Forgive is like apples of gold in pitchers of silver.

Brad and Rebecca Blaisdell
Everlasting Life, Alabama

In this powerful book on forgiveness, the author guides us on a journey to walk us out of the emotional bondage which we have been living. As the author reflects on her own personal life situations, she takes us through the steps of forgiving which leads to freedom. Instead of becoming bitter from unforgiveness, you will be encouraged to become better by learning to forgive.

As you feel God turning those emotional wounds around, you receive a special blessing that will restore your mind, body and soul. Cheryl leaves you with the promise of faith and victory.

Marsha Penrod Damme
California

Do I really have to forgive those who have offended me? If Jesus said to forgive seventy times seven, perhaps there is something we need to consider when we question the need to forgive another when the offence is not our fault. Cheryl, while willing to be candid about her own experiences in life, shares what she has learned about forgiveness, what it does to us when we are not willing to forgive, what it does for us when we do forgive, and how forgiveness helps, not only us, but those involved. If you have a problem with forgiveness, this book is a very excellent source to help you to be able to forgive, or to help you to want to forgive-- for Him, for you.

Jean Hudak Kashella
Pennsylvania

Introduction

Why one more book on forgiving? I asked the Lord the same question. I resisted writing this book for about 4 months, but when I was quiet before Him, He would show me the cover and stir the writings inside of me. His answer to why one more book on forgiving was...because the people who will read this book have not read the other ones. So, I submitted and let Him put this together. I would think I was finished, and then I would encounter three or four situations with people that would remind me of another area.

I am no expert on forgiving. I have not read and studied lots of books on forgiveness and then taken parts of each of them to complete this book. This book is filled with my own personal experiences in the area of forgiveness. I had spent most of my life, I am 53 years old, filled with guilt, regret, resentment, bitterness, anger, and had quite a hard heart, before the Lord began working on me. I have been on this journey of forgiving for the last 8 years. I have spent endless hours before the Lord working on my heart. My past consisted of an alcoholic parent, a troubled home, divorced parents and step parents, molested, rejected, misunderstood, and many other challenges. I made a choice to be given to forgive. I have had many daily opportunities to learn how to forgive from life and people. I have worked on areas of my past while working on my present. I want a better me for the future. I know that hurt people hurt people, and I made the choice to try to change that.

I have experienced great freedom from forgiving. I am not saying that the pictures in our minds of what happened will be forgotten, but definitely the perspective of them will be changed. Just as David chose not to put on Saul's armor before fighting the giant because he was not used to it, I, too, am only writing about what I have experienced and learned. I am always learning as I read His word and encounter challenging situations with people, and spend time with Him about my attitude.

I have learned about forgiveness through being a daughter, a friend, a wife, a mother, a business owner, a neighbor, mother-in-law, and classmate. I have had to forgive people I do not even know or organizations and leaders of churches. I have had to learn to forgive myself for choices and mistakes. I hand you what I have learned and committed to be given to…

As I was putting this book together, I really did not realize how many different levels and angles there were with regards to forgiving. I work on forgiving every single day. Do I always want to? No, I usually have to make myself begin the process, because I know that He steps in and helps me when I do. I have experienced the freedom of choosing to forgive and know that it has been life changing.

Some of the chapters repeat or overlap and have been left in intentionally. Keep reading, I have found that our minds catch things at different times. Allow the Lord to even expand the angles of understanding and do not limit it to just forgiving. This might be a short book, but it contains so much.

I would encourage you to get alone with the Lord and this book. Bring a journal, some worship music, and begin reading with Him. There are a lot of valuable tools, information, and help in this book. He has purposed this book for you, if you are reading it. Share with your family, friends, co-workers and neighbors. You might get mad at some of the chapters because you realize that you were wrong, that is okay, just keep moving forward. God has a purpose for you and this book, and I pray you, too, will be given to forgive all the rest of the days of your life...it can begin today!

You will learn in this book...Forgiveness is not about the other person, it is about you...

CHAPTER 1
Forgive or Not to Forgive

I think nearly every day of our lives we are faced with the choice to forgive or not to forgive people with whom we cross paths. Forgiveness is such a key to our own personal freedom, and yet, at times, it can be the most difficult thing to give in order to receive our freedom. I have come to realize that a simple word misunderstood can cause a hurt.

Fact, people mess up and we get hurt.

Fact, we are not perfect.

Fact, we hurt people like people hurt us.

So what in the world do we do with all the hurts? I wanted to write about a path of forgiveness to keep with you as a tool to freedom in the present and future. This process will be repeated many times in this book; because it works, and we need to be reminded many times until it becomes the way we think.

1. Forgive the person as quickly as possible.

At first, our flesh is not going to want to do this at all. We will not feel like forgiving, and we will be filled with millions of reasons why we should not forgive. We are faced with a choice as soon as we are hurt. The choice is to forgive or not to forgive. Forgiving is not acknowledging that what they did was right. I repeat, forgiving is not acknowledging that what they did was right. Forgiving is the pathway to your personal freedom, and releasing them to the Lord for Him to work with them. Forgiving is a process. We first need to speak the words that you forgive the other person. At first, you will, most likely not feel like it, but when you speak it, it is as if you are reaching out your hand to the Lord to help you. This process is different for everyone. You might have to do this many times, asking the Lord to help you come into agreement with it. That is fine; just keep forgiving until you feel within that you no longer need to speak it. Your very words begin to open the door to freedom.

Our emotions need to forgive, too, so it could take up to seventy times seven to get free of something. However long it takes does not matter; you just need to open the door to the process to allow the Lord in there with you to help. I seem to have a picture of a two year old throwing a tantrum in the middle of a store. There is no reasoning with them in that moment, and they will not listen to anything you have to say. When we fight forgiving another, or refuse to forgive, we are like that two year old in the store, and the Lord watches, but is not able to help us until we calm down and speak that we forgive, and ask Him to help us forgive. It is a pathway to freedom.

2. Ask the Lord to forgive them.

This is what Jesus did on the cross. He asked His Father to forgive them for they did not know what they were doing (Luke 23:34). He left this example in His most painful moment. You do not have to feel this one either, but speaking it begins the process of you releasing them to Him. I know there have been times where I was sure the other person knew what they were doing, but the truth is, they did not. Follow His example in this.

3. Forgive yourself.

If you are dealing with an area of your past where you have not forgiven, you need to forgive yourself. Why? You have most likely taken on what they said, and when you forgive yourself, you again are releasing the agreement that you had with what happened. I usually speak that I forgive myself. You can even speak your own name and proclaim that you forgive yourself. I make it a practice to always forgive myself now to make sure that nothing remains for my future.

4. Ask the Lord to forgive you.

During a challenging moment we are surrounded by thoughts and feelings, and we do not do it all perfectly, or handle the situations perfectly, so it is a good plan to ask the Lord to forgive you for what you thought, said, felt, or anything that wants to set itself up to hinder your relationship with Him.

All of this is for our own freedom. If we have hurt another and we know it, we need to go to them and ask them to forgive us. If another person comes to us and asks us to forgive them, then we need to tell them we forgive them. It releases all the bondage from you and them.

This process is not easy, but it is a good practice for everyday life. It is a choice. Really, the choice is easier to make when you look at it this way; do you want to please the Lord and enable His help, or do you want to continue to hold the other person responsible and push the Lord away, thinking you know better. I think they call that 'pride'. Forgiveness has a bottom line result...relationship. Relationship with Jesus and with others...where do you want to be? Your choice...choose well...

> *Forgiveness is not about the other person, it is about you ...*
>
> **LUKE 23:34**

CHAPTER 2
The Power of Forgiveness

I seem to get many lessons in the power of forgiveness. One day, something happened and I was a bit annoyed inside. I would love to tell you that my first response was to forgive, but it was not. Actually, the thought of forgiving did not even cross my mind. I was only thinking of getting what I was supposed to have gotten. My mind tried to figure out how to get it. I knew not to respond until I did not want my way so badly, so I waited.

I woke up very early to talk to the Lord, and there it was again, that thing, unresolved and annoying me. I could think of nothing else but that and what I would write, and all the other defenses I thought were necessary to get what I wanted. Ever felt that? Of course, we all do at some point in our lives, but, this day, I could not talk to the Lord about anything at all, because my mind would absolutely not stop thinking about this injustice. I finally stopped and asked the Lord what this was really about. Why in the world was I so consumed with this thing? I was offended and asked Him why...What was this really revealing about my heart? I then realized that I needed to forgive.

A wound from my past arose. I forgave the person (with the Lord, not actually calling the person, as this was my issue, not theirs), and I asked the Lord to bring healing to my past in this area. I asked the Lord to forgive me and to forgive them. I repented, and as soon as I did all of this, I was instantaneously free of that which, moments before, was consuming my thoughts. It all lifted. I was then clear to write an email from the proper perspective. WOW!

I have been on this journey of forgiveness for the last 8 years, so I know it is very powerful for my heart and mind. Once I realize that I need to forgive, I do because of the value of it. I do not want anything to separate me from my relationship with the Lord, and unforgiveness is a poison that does just that. I have heard it said that unforgiveness is like you drinking poison and expecting it to harm the other person. Look at the truth of what drinking poison does to the person who drinks it. The enemy loves for us to rise up in choosing not to forgive, and completely tries to convince us that we are justified in our thoughts.

When I first began this journey of forgiving, it was not easy. The more I practiced this, the easier it got because of how I felt once I got free of it. There are times that we hold onto this unforgiveness too long, and everything within us comes into agreement with it, including our emotions. If we sit with it too long, the process takes long to get free. Every part that came into agreement has to let go and forgive. I believe this is what Jesus was talking about when

He told Peter and the others to forgive seventy times seven (Matthew 18:21-35). I, personally, walk through forgiveness like this (from chapter 1):

Lord, I forgive them. Please forgive them, Lord. I forgive myself. I ask that You please forgive me. Please bring healing to every area this has affected.

I do this as many times as it takes until I no longer find it an issue within me. When you can think of that other person without an issue arising within, you are free. In the beginning, it used to take me months to get free, and I would go to the Lord every day and tell Him I need to go through the process again. I told Him I was sorry I had to do this so many times. He told me that He did not have a problem with how many times it took at all. He will listen as much as I need Him to until I am free. I find the process much quicker now, and my insides feel so much better.

Yes, issues still arise, like this one that just did, but I knew what to do, and easily did it, and instantly got free. Remember, the longer you hold onto it, the longer it takes to get free. Just don't quit trying and forgiving...

> ***Forgiveness is not about the other person, it is about you ...***
> **MATTHEW 18:21-35**

CHAPTER 3
The Power of Unforgiveness

A warning to the reader, I am not going to be justifying your reason not to forgive. There is power in unforgiveness, but it is a false power. When we first get hurt by another person, we encounter a type of trauma. It might seem like a small thing, but what happens after it can be small or big and it is our choice. Sometimes it is a choice we do not even realize we can make. Depending on the type or level of the hurt, we can, if we do not choose to forgive, justify and think we have every right not to forgive the other person. They hurt me, so it is not my responsibility to forgive them.

This choice of not forgiving seems, at the time, empowering, and we feel as if we are then in control by not forgiving. They do not deserve it. I will not give that to them. These are all false perceptions of power. The truth is, we are not really having any power over them, and we are allowing the enemy to have power over us. The longer we hold onto this right we think we have, the more power the unforgiveness gains within us. It gains power over our thoughts, our emotions, our choices, our words, our actions, and our relationships. The longer we believe the lie of its empowerment, the more deceived we become. We are blinded to truth. We have rehearsed that hurt within us so many times, every part of our being is convinced that we are right and they are wrong, and they do not deserve to be forgiven.

We will cross paths with this person or hear their name and there it is again, the original hurt being played out to rationalize and justify our choice not to forgive. This can go on for years if we do not deal with it. This power of unforgiveness, then, gains influence over our choices to trust, believe, and protect. It is power alright, but it is like drinking poison. This poison of unforgiveness does not hurt the person we are not giving it to, but is hurting us.

It is like a virus in our computer. We can even infect other people with the words we speak about that person. We continue to try to live life, but get instantly upset when they appear to be happy and life is going great for them and ours is not. This is where we, then, allow the power of unforgiveness to cause us to slander that person. We will avoid them at all costs, and yet, we cannot stop thinking about them and what they did to us. We are stuck. The power of the unforgiveness has control of us while we think we have control over it.

This power destroys the inside of us. All of those feelings of anger, bitterness, and resentment (the fruit of unforgiveness) begin to breakdown our own bodies, just like drinking poison. Our very health is now being controlled by unforgiveness. All of that has to go somewhere, and everything that is not coming out of our mouth, is beginning to breakdown the health of our body. You can deny it, but it is true. I have seen its power, I have experienced its power, and I have been freed from its power.

Let us go back to that moment of the hurt. Let us connect a couple Scriptures to it. 1 Peter 5:8, "Be sober, be vigilant; because your adversary the devil walks about like a roaring lion, seeking whom he may devour." John 10:9-10, "I am the door. If anyone enters by Me, he will be saved, and will go in and out and find pasture. The thief does not come except to steal, and to kill, and to destroy. I have come that they may have life, and that they may have it more abundantly." At the moment we get hurt, we have a choice. We can choose to forgive or not to forgive. There are two doors to choose. One has the adversary, the devil, yelling at the top of his lungs to choose him. He wants to devour you and everything about you. He wants to steal, kill and destroy everything about you. He will lie to you and get you to believe that you have the power when you do not forgive. He will convince you that you have every right. But then, there's Jesus ... He, too, is providing the way through, and He even becomes the door. We just have to choose to forgive, not based on our feelings, not based on who is right and who is wrong, but because we want His help to get through the hurt. We want the true empowerment of "I can do all things through Jesus Christ who strengthens me" power.

The second we tell Jesus we are choosing to forgive them, He is there. He helps our thoughts and emotions. He knows what happened and will take no one's side; He will only side with the truth. He brings understanding. He frees us from the poison. We are submitting to Him and His help is amazing. I have experienced this many times as I encounter a hurt and try to choose as quickly as possible to speak that I am choosing to forgive, and please help my emotions to forgive too. I have felt the emotions of the hurt settle back down and let it go. My reasoning returns. My peace returns. I no longer have any issues when I hear their name or cross paths with them. I am free.

This is great for the hurts we encounter now, but what about the one's that we have allowed to empower us with unforgiveness? It is never too late to begin the forgiving process; it might take longer, but you can get free of it. If you have chronic pain, I would encourage you to spend some time with the Lord and ask Him if it is because of unforgiveness. As He brings a situation or person to your mind, tell Him that you choose to forgive them. Ask Him to forgive them, and then forgive yourself. Ask the Lord to forgive you for holding onto the hurt. Ask Him to help you let it go and completely forgive. Do not stop until you can no longer gain any empowerment in your mind when you think of the hurt. Depending on how long you have held onto this can determine the length of time to get free of it.

I know, sometimes it feels good not to give them the pleasure of our forgiveness. I know that our flesh loves that feeling of control we think we are getting. There is great power in unforgiveness, but the power of it destroys your heart, soul, mind and strength, your emotions, your relationships, and your physical health. Is this really the power we want, the power that destroys us and not them? It is a false, deceptive power only purposed to destroy you.

Forgive as quickly as possible whether you feel like it or not, because chances are, you will not feel like it until He helps you...

> *Forgiveness is not about the other person, it is about you ...*
> **1 PETER 5:8, JOHN 10:9-10**

CHAPTER 4
Our Emotions Count Too

Jesus said to him, "I do not say to you, up to seven times, but up to seventy times seven (Matthew 18:22)." Jesus is answering the question that Peter asked about how many times he was to forgive. The Lord continues to teach me about forgiveness, and every time it seems to come back to the words He spoke to Peter. In the world in which we live, we get hurt, and unfortunately, at times, hurt others. What we personally do with these hurts affects how we think, hear, feel, and make decisions in our future. How many times do you encounter having to forgive? May I encourage you to keep forgiving until you feel free within from the offense...

For the last 3-1/2 years, I have been on a journey of learning how to forgive. I have had to learn how to forgive things and people of my past, while at the same time, forgiving people in my present. It seems that forgiving others and asking for forgiveness is becoming a daily way of life. At the beginning, I did not like to forgive. I felt, personally, that when I forgave someone, it meant that what they did to me was okay, and so I resisted. I then progressed into the ability, or willingness, to forgive, and tried to learn to let it go after I forgave, and every time the emotions of the situation rose up, I tried to ignore them and not allow my emotions or mind to think about them because I had forgiven. But it seemed to be a continuous struggle...

I then progressed into forgiving the person every time the emotions rose up within me. I was not ignoring them anymore, and I would find myself going to the Lord, telling Him I need to forgive again. I felt bad inside that I had to keep going back to forgive, and wondered if maybe I was not doing it right. One day the Lord told me that He did not care how many times I had to come to Him to forgive the one situation. I was to keep doing it until I felt free from the emotions too. This became a way of life for me. I found great comfort and safety going to the Lord repeatedly with the emotions of forgiving as they rose up. It was as if I was sitting in a hot tub and every part of my being just relaxed and felt safe as I went to the Lord again and again for the same offense.

I found this very interesting. We have the emotions from a particular situation, and they, too, need to forgive. Think about it...for me, those emotions would bring me back to re-living the situation, and, if I was not careful, I would stay in that situation and think about how to fight back, or speak words, maybe in anger, of how I really felt about what they did. This path usually leads to resentment and bitterness, but not healing. But the emotions do rise up, and so, continually going to the Lord with them and forgiving repeatedly allowed those emotions to connect to forgiveness, too.

I want to propose today that another possible way to look at the words of Jesus when He is speaking to Peter above, could also come to mean that in each situation where we are faced with forgiving, it could take us up to seventy times seven times of forgiving to finally be free of the situation. Each area of our emotions that connected to the time of the hurt also needs to connect to the forgiveness. It might seem like a lot of work, but when you practice this, you become aware of every time the emotions surface, and you simply forgive them, ask the Lord to forgive them; and forgive yourself, and keep going on with your day. Eventually, the emotions stop rising up and it is done. There really is freedom in this process and great comfort from the Lord. We have freedom to forgive as many times as it takes for all of us from within to come into agreement with it. If you have many people to forgive, then in your mind line them up and begin forgiving...give your emotions the benefit of forgiving, too.

I got to experience this in action with another person several years ago when my daughter experienced a surprise breakup with a guy she was dating. She had no idea it was coming, so it knocked her over. It happened right before a weekend when my husband and son were going camping, so it was just she and I for the weekend. I gave her permission to talk about it whenever it surfaced. I continued to remind her to forgive as quickly as possible. We went on walks, and as we were walking, all of a sudden she would talk about it again, and she would forgive him, ask the Lord to forgive him, and she forgave herself. After about five times of doing this, she began to experience freedom. It was as if I could see ropes falling off of her. She did not realize it, but she had changed little things about herself to please him. As she forgave, those little things got untied and she liked them again. It was crazy to witness this. By the end of the weekend she was completely free of this breakup, and her heart was completely healed. All of her emotions and thoughts were allowed to forgive. It was much easier and a faster process because of how quickly we addressed it. *(Take note: this is a great way to walk out a hurt with another person who is stuck.)*

As I have written, we all need to forgive, our heart, soul, mind, and emotions. Allow them to all forgive and don't stop until it does not come up anymore inside of you...

> ***Forgiveness is not about the other person, it is about you ...***
>
> **MATTHEW 18.22**

CHAPTER 5
A Friend Named Guilt

It was another early morning of wrestling with a long time friend named Guilt. Guilt is one of those friends that remains inside of me privately and controls my perception in many areas. I do not like guilt, and yet, there it is day after day. I do not want to feel this way, and I have not been able to figure out how to get free of its control because the situation I am feeling guilty about continues to be there, and is not resolved, and cannot ever be resolved, so I wrestle with guilt.

Thirteen years ago, my dad died of a heart attack while on vacation. It was so sudden and was such a deep, deep loss. My relationship with my dad had only been reconciled for the last ten years of his life, and I will forever be grateful for those ten years, but it still hurts as I go through big events in my life and in the lives of my children. He is missed. Even as I write this the tears are streaming down my face. If you have experienced this type of loss, then you understand what I am writing...

My dad was married to his third wife for those last ten years of his life, and so, at his passing, we tried to maintain a relationship with her and care for her. We did a good job of it for the first four years. But when the Lord called us to shut down our business, sell everything, and attend ministry school, we moved across the United States to South Carolina. The move created such a distance our relationship soon began to falter. She did not understand our decision or faith, and I am sure she felt abandoned. I am not sure I handled it all the correct way and could have done more to keep the relationship alive, but I was being taken into a season of brokenness, so I was pulled to please the Lord first, and that decision created many challenging relationships. My dad's wife became quite bitter with me.

She then began to show signs of dementia. This only seemed to compound the bitterness and resentment because her filter system seemed to be the first to go. By filter system I mean that place within each of us where we think before we speak. So, I would get quite an ear full at various visits. No matter how many times I said I was sorry, it would not get resolved. So, the distance grew bigger.

She found another male friend and became part of his family. I was grateful because they were very good to her and loved and cared for her. The guilt inside of me grew. Through all of this I wrestled with...my dad's estate and his personal belongings were under her control... am I maintaining a relationship with her just to eventually receive my inheritance? So many struggles and emotions and questions...the distance grew and so did the guilt.

What would my dad think? What are the members of the other family thinking about me? The distance and guilt grew inside of me...

The beginning of last year, I began praying for understanding hearts in each of the members of this other family, as they now were in charge of her care and estate, as she now was in a home with Alzheimer's. She had told them, over the years, of my failings, so her resentment had been picked up by them. The guilt inside of me grew...

I received an unexpected email from the people caring for her, and they began to include me in the selling of her home and other things. I was encouraged and even went and visited her, but if you are at all familiar with Alzheimer's, you know the patient has trouble remembering anything, which in one way was good, and in another way was bad. So my guilt would not go away. Morning after morning, there I was feeling guilty over how I handled things, and now my lack of visitation, as I live 2-1/2 hours away. A visit with her is very difficult and she doesn't even remember that you visited. So, inside of me is this place that wrestles with what to do. It is painful to carry this, and I have not been able to get rid of this guilt.

One morning, the Lord brought up the struggle inside of me. He asked me who I was trying to please. Am I trying to please my stepmother or the people? I know there is really no way to please my stepmother anymore, so my answer was the people. He showed me I was wrestling with trying to please people who do not know the whole situation from my side of it, nor do they understand my internal struggle with feeling so guilty about where this whole thing is at the moment. He showed me my guilt for what it really was. He asked me to give the guilt to Him. He told me I needed to forgive myself. I forgave myself and am going to continue to forgive myself until this guilt is gone.

I saw I was not forgiving myself as a way of punishing myself for the guilt I was feeling. I was trying to please these people to help my guilt, and really, there is nothing I can do that is going to please them to the level of acceptance that I would need to feel free of this guilt. Only He knew how to free me. Only He knows all of my choices and thoughts and actions through all of this. My focus should be on pleasing Him through all of this because He knows me best. So my journey began by freeing myself of this hidden guilt that can only be resolved by forgiving myself and doing what He shows me to do.

Guilt from our past choices hinders us in so many ways. It can keep us from receiving blessings or appreciating them because it works on convincing us that we do not deserve them. Guilt can hinder us from walking in the fullness of who we are and can be...are you carrying guilt? Do you need to forgive yourself? I began receiving much clarity about the subtle controls of guilt as I began to forgive myself...

> *Forgiveness is not about the other person, it is about you ...*
>
> **COLOSSIANS 3:12-16**

CHAPTER 6
Influence of the Past

I was in a friendship with a person for several years. We were what I would consider very good friends. The friendship had its struggles, but it seemed to keep enduring. I found myself getting hurt feelings many times, and yet, I never really could find the courage to talk about it, so, those hurts became buried inside of me. I cannot tell you that each time it happened I completely understood what was happening, so to discuss it might have been pointless at the time. As a result, they piled up inside of me. Did I see I needed to forgive? No, inside I felt I was right and they would not understand. I never thought these hurts needed to be connected to forgiveness.

Well, about seven years ago, the Lord put an end to the friendship. One morning I had a vision of His hand coming down in between the two of us, and we were sitting with our backs to each other. If I did not get this message, I had another vision of a computer screen and the Lord unplugging it, and I actually heard the sound of the computer shutting off after it was unplugged. I got the message and the communication was stopped between the two of us. To tell you the truth, I did not understand why this needed to happen. I was devastated for many months at the loss of this friendship.

A couple years after that, the Lord started showing me my heart about this person. He showed it to me in many different ways. I would hear of their success, or someone would be talking about them, or even invite me to a function they were having, and this thing inside of me would rise up. So, I began the journey of forgiveness with the Lord. Every day I would sit down and say, "Okay Lord, I do not have a good attitude about this person. I need to forgive them. I choose to forgive them. I ask You to forgive them. I ask You to forgive me. Help me to forgive them." I did this day after day as things would pop into my head about something that happened or that was said. After about a month of doing this every day, I told the Lord I was sorry I had to keep coming to Him day after day, forgiving over and over. He told me He was fine with it and He would listen as many times as it took for me to be free of it.

I will admit, for the longest time, I was forgiving just because I knew I should, but inside I continued to think it was really their fault and they should be apologizing to me. I began to recognize when something would happen and I felt it again. I would sit with Him and forgive again. He would bring a situation or conversation to mind, and I would feel it, and back to Him I would go. I did this for two years straight.

INFLUENCE OF THE PAST

I had a dream where I was hugging this person, and once again, I felt the love for them. I took that to mean I was free, so I wrote to them. I wrote that I was sorry, and went into a little bit of detail about my process and heart. I did not blame them for any of it, just finally had the courage and understanding to write about my side of it. Their response triggered a few more things inside of me, and so, I went back to the Lord to work on my heart. I forgave them for their response and continued this process until it was not coming up in my thoughts anymore.

I would see a post on Facebook and there it was again, inside of me, and so, I went back to working on forgiving again. Finally, three years later I saw a post of an amazing opportunity they were given to do, which happened to be something I hope one day I will be given to do, and all that I felt was joy for them. I was shocked. I was really happy for them. I was able to pray for them and thank the Lord for the opportunity given to them and how that is going to change their very life. I will admit I did pray for them in the past, but it was something like this, "Lord, reveal to them their heart and how wrong they treated me. Open up their understanding and give them eyes to see." But now my heart and mind are rejoicing and excited for them. I am free. My heart is clear. What changed? Every part of me finally has forgiven...this freedom is rich and deep.

How is your heart? Do you hear someone's name and something rises up inside of you? Do you cross paths with someone from your past and then the rest of the day you are reliving the hurt, and rationalizing and justifying the wrong? Do you see them and avoid them at all costs? Do you see a post or picture and something stirs you up inside that is not good? This is unforgiveness...I, personally, did not want to forgive at the beginning. I did not feel like I needed to, but I did. He is patient with us as we try...He will listen to us as we try and try and try...

Is there someone you need to forgive?

> ***Forgiveness is not about the other person, it is about you ...***
>
> ***COLOSSIANS 3:12-16***

CHAPTER 7
Will You For Me?

A while back, I got some news from someone close to me about their health. It was potentially bad news. After I got the news, I noticed I really did not feel anything inside about it, and I should have. As I sought the Lord about my heart response to this news, He showed me a place inside my heart I had hardened. I was surprised at this discovery. How could it be there? I have spent hours forgiving this person.

The Lord showed me there was a place within my heart that was holding out the last place of forgiving until this person took responsibility for all the hurts they had caused me while I was growing up. I was not totally aware of this place, but as He showed me, I realized it was there. I was holding on to this last bit of forgiving until they took responsibility.

As I looked at it with the Lord, He said to me, "What if you never get what you are wanting? What if you never hear them take responsibility for what they have done? Will you forgive them for Me?" I thought about what He was saying. He explained that forgiving for Him was honoring them and Him. This was shaking up all of my thoughts, feelings, and emotions. I finally was able to tell the Lord yes. I would forgive them for Him, not for them, but for Him. So, I forgave them in that moment and let that little place, where I had stood my ground in my heart, go. I want my relationship with Him over being right or having the last word. I felt it release.

Then, He began to show me person after person to whom I had done this very thing. I was shocked at this discovery. He showed me people who had broken my trust, and I had set up a place in my heart where I was no longer going to trust them. He explained that He is not asking me to trust them, but to trust Him with them and the outcome of what happened. I need to trust Him with the responsibility of what happened. I forgave them for Him. As He brought each person by name to me, I looked at what I had done with their hurt, and chose to forgive them for Him. I was not forgiving them for them, and I was no longer going to hold out for that last place of them coming to me and taking responsibility for what they did. Some of these were deep and I had been holding onto them for many years. I forgave them all for Him, one by one. I felt the control and protecting let go, and I trusted Him with them.

I realized that I was holding onto this last place and I did not trust Him. It was a bit of pride and entitlement mixed together and holding on very tight. We do this. We may not be completely aware of this choice that we make, but if we are not mindful of it, we do it.

This is not an easy thing to face. I would encourage you to take some time and sit with the Lord and ask Him if there are people in your life that you, too, are holding on to unforgiveness until they take responsibility. Then wait for Him to show you. Be brave. Be real with Him. I have had many discussions with the Lord about why I think I have a right to hold onto this or that. He always comes to the same conclusion. Forgiveness is about me and my relationship with Him and not the other person at all. The enemy loves for us to think it is about them. The enemy loves for us to hold onto this hurt or wrong that has been done against us. He knows that when we hold onto it, relationships remain broken, and our heart gets a little more hardened toward the ways of God each time. The enemy makes it about the other person and the Lord makes it about us and our heart. Do we want to hold onto our right not to forgive at the price of holding back a place from God? I did not.

I ask you again to be brave to ask, face what is within that He shows you, and then forgive them for Him...not them, Him.

After all the tests, it turned out not to be bad news. God used it to show me my own heart and I listened and got free...

He asks you, "Will you forgive them for Me?"

> *Forgiveness is not about the other person,
> it is about you ...*
>
> *MATTHEW 18:21-35*

CHAPTER 8
The Example of a Parent

Mom: Tell your sister you are sorry.

Son: But I'm not!

Mom: Tell her you are sorry anyway.

Son: But I didn't do anything wrong.

Mom: Tell your sister you are sorry.

Son: Sorry...

Mom: Tell your brother you forgive him.

Daughter: I forgive you.

This above situation happened many times in our home when my two children were younger. Did it accomplish true forgiveness? Is this training them to take responsibility for their actions? What do you do when they do not feel they have done anything wrong? As a parent, we are constantly placed in this position of mediation, if not with our own children, then that with one of our children and a child from another home. This forgiveness process is not just for grown-ups.

In Proverbs 22:6, "Train up a child in the way he should go, and when he is old he will not depart from it." Does this apply to forgiveness? Are we supposed to train our children to forgive? How in the world do we train our children to do this, when we ourselves have not fully learned this? Maybe you are better at this than I, but for me, I started on this forgiveness process eight years ago, and I am 53 years old. My children, at this moment, are 26 and 20. You do the math on this; they were not very young when I began working on my own forgiveness from my past. You cannot force someone to say they are sorry and mean it, but we, as parents, surely do try at times. You also cannot make someone forgive you, no matter how much we say we are sorry or try to explain. So, what is our responsibility in this "train up a child in the way he should go" in regards to forgiveness?

To me, it is modeling it each day. When I mess up, I try to go to them and tell them I am sorry. I had no right to do or say what I said. I will do this in person, if it is possible. If it is not, then I will call, text, or write an email. I try to do this as quickly as possible. First, I am teaching them to take responsibility for their actions by taking care of mine. Second, I am teaching them how to apologize and what it looks like. The more I work on my own heart, as I have written in this book, the easier it is getting to model this to my family.

THE EXAMPLE OF A PARENT

I had not intended to write a chapter about this topic, but I am walking through something with one of my children and realize it needs to be included. Eight years ago, my husband and I shut down our business, sold nearly everything we had, and moved our family across the United States to go to ministry school. We spent a year in South Carolina and then spent 18 months outside of the United States. We came back to our home in South Carolina for a couple more years and then moved back to Northern California. This process was difficult for our family, and our son, in particular, has not appreciated our choices to do all of this. Several times a year, and sometimes even more than that, he lets us know that we ruined his life. He wants nothing to do with God and is angry. No matter what we say or how much we explain why we did what we did, he refuses to let it go. It is very difficult to hear his words, but I continue to listen and then go to prayer. He does not understand why we would do that to him. He is twenty years old and has been upset with us and God for the last 8 years.

As a parent, I feel guilty about how he feels about our life. I think we have a very good life, but he somehow feels cheated. That guilt is not fun for a parent to carry, and it influences certain choices and decisions we make or do not make. We constantly are trying to make up for what we did, but it is never good enough. There does not seem to be any reasoning with him. So, as I sat with the Lord begging Him to tell me or show me what I can do to help him, He reminded me of what I wrote about in the chapter titled, "Will You for Me?". In walking through my own hurts from my childhood, what I really wanted was for my parent to just take responsibility for the choices they made that hurt me and tell me they were sorry. I will admit that when He showed me what I needed to do, I did not jump on board right away. I heard, yet again, my reasons and rationalization that I have told him over and over again. I knew that the Lord was showing me what to do through my experience. I understood how it feels not to be heard or considered. I understood what I needed to do. So, I wrote him a short email asking him that I hoped one day he would be able to forgive us for hurting him. We did not intentionally do it, but it did hurt him and for that we are sorry.

Yes, I will admit that I just want to move on from all of this and forget about it. I cannot change our choice and I cannot change our lives in the past. But, he is stuck there. That twelve year old boy was deeply hurt by our choice. Whether we can see value in our decision does not help make up for the hurt and devastation the little boy remembers and feels. At the moment, he resents us and does not respect us. But, I trust God with him and the process it is going to take to get him back. I, as his mom, am giving him what I longed to receive from my parents, an apology without excuses or justifications or reasons. I am still walking this out, it does not get any more up to date and current than this. If He wants this in the book, then there must be other parents out there who have made decisions that have hurt their children, and maybe they are wondering why their children act the way they do. I pray this helps you and your family...

God modeled and gave forgiveness...He is our example that we, as parents, know how to model and give forgiveness, too. Don't hold onto your child's failures or mistakes. If they apologize, forgive them and let it go. Don't bring it up in the next confrontation or disagreement...let it go. Ask God to help you and He will...

> *Forgiveness is not about the other person, it is about you ...*
>
> **PROVERBS 22:6**

CHAPTER 9
Generational Influences

Do you ever wonder about why you think what you think? Do you ever wonder about why you have an attitude about something or prejudice? I was recognizing an internal wrestling match with myself in a particular area, and I had no idea why I was thinking this way. I did not recall anything happening to stir my thinking in this direction. It actually was not a logical way to think about the situation, and when I really looked at it, I did not even believe it, and yet, I was thinking this and it was influencing me. Why?

I went to the Lord and asked Him why I was thinking this way? It was exhausting me. He then began to show me my dad. He recalled memories of times where my dad was thinking and speaking these very things. Then He showed me that his father did this, too. It was generational. It was not a positive attitude. It definitely was not the way the Lord thinks and did not line up with His Word. Exodus 34:7, "keeping mercy for thousands, forgiving iniquity and transgression and sin, by no means clearing the guilty, visiting the iniquity of the fathers upon the children and the children's children to the third and the fourth generation" shows us there are things that happened or were said without our knowledge that have an influence on us now. This can feel impossible to figure out, or we can even deny that it is true, but when we partner with Him and trust His timing to show us and use situations around us to make us aware of it, it is real and good.

When I was eleven or twelve years old, one of my parents was very troubled with their life and tried to commit suicide. I was home when this happened, and I found them and went to get help for them. It was a traumatic moment in my life. We did not know the Lord so this event in my life never got addressed as I was growing up. When my daughter was around this same age, she wrestled with thoughts of suicide. I could not figure out why she was struggling with this, so I prayed and prayed for her. Then, when my son got to this same age, he, too, wrestled with the same thought. It got my attention. I went to the Lord and asked Him what in the world was going on. He began to show me how this event in my life opened a door to theirs. It seems obvious once He shows me, but when you are living life these types of connections do not always connect. But when both of these situations above were revealed to me, this is what I did...

I went before the Lord in prayer and thanked Him for my parents. I thanked Him for their care and provision they gave me. I, then, forgave them for what they said and did. I asked the Lord to please forgive them, and I asked the Lord to forgive me. I, then, asked the Lord to close the doors

GENERATIONAL INFLUENCES

to the thoughts, the sins, and words these created for me and for my children and future generations. I, then, asked the Lord to bless our family line in the past, present, and future. I asked Him to renew the generations and renew our minds to His Word. In the case of the first example, I went back a few generations beyond my parents, and even went back on the suicide attempt as well. I want all of these doors closed for me and my children and all of the generations after me.

Are you noticing a pattern of thoughts or situations happening in your life and you are wondering why? I would encourage you to take some time to ask the Lord what it is. I have worked with people in this area, and sometimes they discover things they never knew about. Use caution if the people are still alive. It might not be necessary to go to the people and confront them. Keep it about you and the Lord. Work on the repairing with prayer and love. I have not gone to my parents about this, as it was not about them, but what had been created. They were doing the best they could at that time in their life, and I am grateful for their care for me. I cannot change the past but I can change the present that is now being written and is influencing my future and the future of generations to come. Most of the time, it is wisdom to keep these types of revelations between you and the Lord.

Forgiveness process again is this...

1. Thank Him.
2. Forgive them.
3. Ask the Lord to forgive them.
4. Ask the Lord to forgive you.

5. Ask the Lord to close the doors.
6. Bless them and the future generations.
7. Keep it between you and the Lord, unless He makes it crystal clear that you are to go to the person about it.

It is never too late to do this...

> ***Forgiveness is not about the other person, it is about you ...***
>
> ***EXODUS 34:7***

CHAPTER 10
Those Repeat Offenders

What do we do with the people in our lives who continually seem to hurt us with their words, actions, choices, behavior, or other various things? We have worked on the forgiveness process for the past, but the daily things, what about those? As hard as it gets sometimes, we still have to find it within ourselves to forgive them. I, personally, have a few of these situations I live with on a daily basis, and I fight an array of emotions to make the choice to forgive. Maybe it is a co-worker, a fellow student, a spouse, a child, a friend or a relative; it is all the same in regards to forgiving. I have not found any verse in the Bible that gives us a reason we do not have to forgive. I know how important it is to keep a short account and forgive quickly.

I fight all of the mental battles of:

Why do I have to be the one who always has to forgive? What about them?

Or...They just continue to do the same thing over and over and I am tired of forgiving them...

Or...What is the use?

Or...They are not working on their heart, why do I have to work on mine?

Or...I am tired of forgiving and getting hurt!

If you are in situations like this, you might even have a few of your own thoughts that are not here. We get tired of forgiving. This is why we have to be given to it. It has to become our first choice before all of the emotions begin to give their opinion of what we should or should not do.

We cannot allow ourselves to make this about them and their choices. Forgiveness is about us and only us and our heart health.

I was talking to someone the other day, and I explained that every time we feel our emotions or something inside of us elevate, we need to forgive, just like the indicator for an earthquake. We need to recognize the moment we are hurt and inside forgive them, ask the Lord to forgive them, and ask the Lord to forgive us, and then ask Him to help us through this. This is the process to keeping a short account in the area of forgiving and being fully given to forgive.

I am absolutely not going to say this is easy. It is not. As we know, if we do not choose this, we will gain an attitude that leads to resentment and bitterness, and that choice will do us no good, but only distances us from the Lord.

Forgiveness is not about the other person, it is about you ...

MATTHEW 18:21-22

CHAPTER 11
For a Future Time

About eight years ago, I encountered a family member who was not happy with me. So much so, they stopped talking to me completely. It hurt and I tried and tried. It not only hurt me but my children, too. The point is not what happened, but what I did with the choice of this other person.

I worked on my heart, just like all of the chapters have said. I had to work on it very hard and for many hours.

A few months ago, my daughter got married. Prior to the wedding, I was praying that somehow the Lord would give this person an understanding heart and they would come to the wedding. If I had not been working on my heart and mind for all of these years, I would not have been able to pray this, nor would I have wanted it. My daughter was a little challenged with the thought of this. She, too, needed to work on her heart. She was upset for me. I encouraged her to begin to work on her heart and to forgive, so that if they were to come, she would be ready to embrace them and be excited to see them.

This is a short chapter, but very important. Sometimes, we forgive people in preparation for a future time when we will see them. We need to prepare for a time when they might come and say they are sorry and ask for our forgiveness. We are responsible for us and our heart, and sometimes it takes years for people to come back, but be ready for when they do. This person did come to the wedding, and when I saw them, I gave them the biggest hug I had to give. I was so excited they came. They never did apologize, but I did not care, because God had worked on my heart and mind. My daughter, too, was excited to see them.

> ***Forgiveness is not about the other person, it is about you ...***
>
> ***2 CORINTHIANS 2:10-11***

CHAPTER 12
Don't Forget to Forgive God

Life happens, sometimes the way we planned it, and sometimes it is not how we thought it would go. In these moments when we find ourselves in the 'not zone', we need to be mindful of what we do with them. If we are not careful, we will or can blame God for not coming through for us. It is in the moments when life did not turn out the way we thought, that, potentially, we can begin to break down our trust in God.

In 2005, the Lord asked my husband and I to shut down our business that we had had for 19 years, to sell everything we had, and go to ministry school in South Carolina; we were living in California at the time. We did as He asked and left everything we knew, took our two children and relocated on the other side of the United States. We were there for a year, and then, following the direction of the Lord again, we left South Carolina and travelled to New Zealand for 4 months, and ultimately, to Australia for 14 months. I am simplifying the enormous steps of faith to make all these moves. This season of our life was the most difficult season any of us have ever experienced, and we would not want to do it again. Everything that could be shaken was shaken.

When we returned from this shaking, we felt the Lord was going to put us in full-time ministry. We were sure we went through all of that and had sacrificed everything so we now would be employed by a church. Surely that was His plan for us. Guess what? It did not happen. We struggled, and my husband found work here and there. What happened to the plan, God? My perception of what was supposed to happen, and obviously, God's perception of what was going to happen were totally different. I had a choice, be angry with God or forgive Him. Yes, there are times we need to forgive God. Not for Him, but for us. We can hold this against Him, but we are totally wrong. We can get angry with Him because we think He abandoned us after all we had done and given up for Him. Maybe we are angry He did not answer our prayers.

The truth is, this could have been His plan all along, and we had the wrong perception of the outcome. I think the Israelites struggled with this, too. God took them into the wilderness with a promise of a land flowing with milk and honey, but everything they encountered was anything but that promise. It was only a 13-day journey, but it turned into 40 years because of their hearts toward God and their attitude. He took them into the wilderness to prepare them and get Egypt out of them. They had a different perception of what being delivered looked like. Just like us, we can be angry with God about how our life turned out. We need to spend some time forgiving God, and also, forgiving ourselves. I think we stay in the place of the wilderness until we stop blaming God for where we are and discover and embrace where He has us and the process we are in.

Maybe your life is not as extreme as ours, but what about college plans or businesses that we started thinking God wanted us to do and they failed. What about marriages that did not work and we were sure God put it together? What about our children making choices that cause them harm and we have been praying for their protection? What about...you fill in the blank. Do you have something? I encourage you to sit with God and forgive Him. When you do, many of your struggles, anger, bitterness, guilt, resentment, and regret will begin to change. I know, for me, I began to get His perspective on life. I realized that Australia was our Egypt. I realized ministry is our daily life, not a position. Do you need to forgive God?

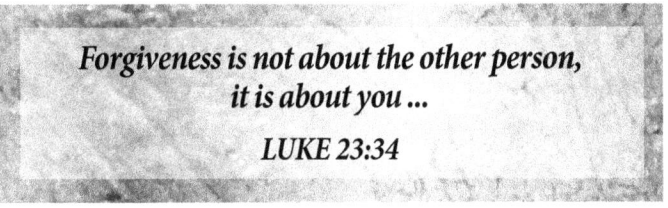

Forgiveness is not about the other person, it is about you ...

LUKE 23:34

CHAPTER 13
Forgive Yourself Too

We come to the last chapter of this book. How are you doing? I do hope you have worked through some forgiveness and are experiencing freedom. It is a daily choice to forgive those around us. This book would not be complete without addressing what I have found to be the most important part of forgiveness. We need to forgive ourselves. Many times this is forgotten. I have included it many times in the chapters prior, and as part of the process, but I have found it to be life changing to forgive myself.

It may seem simple, but many times I have experienced and witnessed this to be the toughest of all to do. Somehow, inside of us, we have a challenge with forgiving ourselves for mistakes or things we have done that we know are not pleasing to the Lord, or choices we have made. We somehow feel we deserve to feel this guilt inside or feel awful. Think about it.

When we choose to do this, it is as if we are saying the Lord's forgiveness is not good enough. We feel we need to be punished, and so we do not feel we deserve to be forgiven. The truth is, we are not any different from the people we are to forgive. We are in the same boat as they are. There are people in our lives who are difficult to forgive, and usually we are at the front of the line.

Do you feel guilt? Do you feel not good enough? Do you feel stuck? Do you know that you have not forgiven yourself? I would encourage you to forgive you. You might have to just make the choice and speak the words. You might not feel like it, but start the process as you have with everyone else, and then ask the Lord to help you. You will be amazed at how freeing this can be.

All of the internal punishment you have been applying to yourself by feeling like you do not deserve this or that, will begin shifting how you think. I have made it a practice to try to forgive myself every day. This might seem excessive, but I believe we do things throughout the day that we are not pleased with, or feel we could do better, and making the choice to forgive ourselves allows us to start fresh.

His forgiveness is enough; we do not need to punish ourselves for the rest of our lives. Pray something like this...Lord Jesus, I choose today to forgive myself, and I ask You to please forgive me for holding onto this and feeling or believing that I deserve to be punished, and for not accepting Your forgiveness. Please help me to completely forgive myself. In Jesus Name, Amen!

"If you forgive the sins of any, they are forgiven them, if you retain the sins of any they are retained" (John 20:23). Apply this to you...you are included in the 'any'. We do not need to retain them inside of us; He did not make us that way.

> ***Forgiveness is not about the other person, it is about you ...***
>
> **JOHN 20:23**

CHAPTER 14
Concluding Points

- Most of the time when we get offended it is because we have unforgiveness somewhere inside of us...take the next step when the offense happens and ask the Lord what it is about. You will, most likely, discover that at some point you got hurt by someone and you chose not to forgive...unforgiveness leaves us vulnerable to future offenses ...

- A marriage is slowly destroyed by unforgiveness one day at a time ... if we allow it ...

- Do not allow the enemy to convince you that the other person has to say they are sorry before you can forgive. Remember that it is not about them, but you. We cannot change the other person, we can only change us (with God's help).

- Guilt, regret, anger, resentment, bitterness, and even impatience are all symptoms of unforgiveness. Be aware of it inside of yourself, and also, in other people. When we recognize this is what is going on inside the other person, it is easier to forgive them, as they do not know what they are doing (Jesus' example).

- Remember, this is a process of learning and choosing. I have given you eight years of my journey, so allow yourself to learn it. Partner with the Holy Spirit each day. Do not go digging for who you need to forgive, let the Lord direct it. Just give Him permission and He will bring dreams, situations, messages, and memories to help you. Being given to forgive is a daily choice. I have made it my life purpose, and I am intentional about it, but it is still not easy, at times.

- Do not allow the little daily things to build up. The little misunderstanding or tone of voice from another person, forgive them immediately inside of you. I promise this will make a difference. Those little things add up very quickly, and soon anger, bitterness, resentment, and impatience have made their way into your response, attitudes, and choices.

- If you are having trouble, or recognize resistance inside of you in regards to another person, and you cannot bring yourself to be appreciative or say thank you, this is a sign that you need to forgive that person. This is also a sign to recognize in other people and their lack of appreciation toward you. Forgive them.

CONCLUDING POINTS

- I hope to, one day, get to the point where my absolute first response is always to forgive. I am not there yet, but it is my goal.

- Sometimes forgiving is a process that needs to be repeated many times, especially on deep hurts of the past. Keep forgiving until it does not come up again. Learn to pay attention to what is going on inside of you.

- In the chapter of, 'Forgive Yourself Too', where I forgive for Him, after doing this I began to notice that my heart and attitude toward this person had totally changed. I no longer had this place inside of me that I had to wrestle with. The conversations and relationship with this person have improved, both ways, significantly. What was inside of me before was influencing the relationship and I did not recognize that. Proverbs 4:23

- If we wait until we feel like forgiving, we will most likely never forgive...make the choice to forgive then the desire comes after ...

- I would encourage you to read through the book again with the Holy Spirit, and you will be amazed at the areas you missed the first time through. There are many layers to this book, may we all discover them all and more ...

> *Forgiveness is not about the other person, it is about you ...*
> **LUKE 6:37-38**

CHAPTER 15
Scriptures

Luke 23:34

[34] Then Jesus said, "Father, forgive them, for they do not know what they do."And they divided His garments and cast lots.

Matthew 18:21-35

[21] Then Peter came to Him and said, "Lord, how often shall my brother sin against me, and I forgive him? Up to seven times?"

[22] Jesus said to him, "I do not say to you, up to seven times, but up to seventy times seven. [23] Therefore the kingdom of heaven is like a certain king who wanted to settle accounts with his servants. [24] And when he had begun to settle accounts, one was brought to him who owed him ten thousand talents. [25] But as he was not able to pay, his master commanded that he be sold, with his wife and children and all that he had, and that payment be made. [26] The servant therefore fell down before him,

saying, 'Master, have patience with me, and I will pay you all.' ²⁷ Then the master of that servant was moved with compassion, released him, and forgave him the debt.

²⁸ "But that servant went out and found one of his fellow servants who owed him a hundred denarii; and he laid hands on him and took him by the throat, saying, 'Pay me what you owe!' ²⁹ So his fellow servant fell down at his feet and begged him, saying, 'Have patience with me, and I will pay you all.' ³⁰ And he would not, but went and threw him into prison till he should pay the debt. ³¹ So when his fellow servants saw what had been done, they were very grieved, and came and told their master all that had been done. ³² Then his master, after he had called him, said to him, 'You wicked servant! I forgave you all that debt because you begged me. ³³ Should you not also have had compassion on your fellow servant, just as I had pity on you?' ³⁴ And his master was angry, and delivered him to the torturers until he should pay all that was due to him.

³⁵ "So My heavenly Father also will do to you if each of you, from his heart, does not forgive his brother his trespasses."

1 Peter 5:8

⁸ Be sober, be vigilant; because your adversary the devil walks about like a roaring lion, seeking whom he may devour.

John 10:9-10

⁹ I am the door. If anyone enters by Me, he will be saved, and will go in and out and find pasture. ¹⁰ The thief does not come except to steal, and to kill, and to destroy. I have come that they may have life, and that they may have it more abundantly.

Colossians 3:12-16

¹² Therefore, as the elect of God, holy and beloved, put on tender mercies, kindness, humility, meekness, longsuffering; ¹³ bearing with one another, and forgiving one another, if anyone has a complaint against another; even as Christ forgave you, so you also must do. ¹⁴ But above all these things put on love, which is the bond of perfection.¹⁵ And let the peace of God rule in your hearts, to which also you were called in one body; and be thankful. ¹⁶ Let the word of Christ dwell in you richly in all wisdom, teaching and admonishing one another in psalms and hymns and spiritual songs, singing with grace in your hearts to the Lord.

Proverbs 22:6

⁶ Train up a child in the way he should go, And when he is old he will not depart from it.

Exodus 34:7

⁷ keeping mercy for thousands, forgiving iniquity and transgression and sin, by no means clearing the guilty, visiting the iniquity of the fathers upon the children and the children's children to the third and the fourth generation."

2 Corinthians 2:10-11

[10] Now whom you forgive anything, I also forgive. For if indeed I have forgiven anything, I have forgiven that one for your sakes in the presence of Christ, [11] lest Satan should take advantage of us; for we are not ignorant of his devices.

John 20:23

[23] If you forgive the sins of any, they are forgiven them; if you retain the sins of any, they are retained."

Proverbs 4:23

[23] Keep your heart with all diligence, For out of it spring the issues of life.

Luke 6:37-38

[37] Judge not, and you shall not be judged. Condemn not, and you shall not be condemned. Forgive, and you will be forgiven. [38] Give, and it will be given to you: good measure, pressed down, shaken together, and running over will be put into your bosom. For with the same measure that you use, it will be measured back to you.

Do You Need Jesus?

If for some reason you have received this book and you do not know Jesus as your personal Savior, I want you to know that you can. There is nothing that you have done that He will not forgive, if you ask Him. Just repeat this simple prayer to begin your amazing journey with Jesus.

Dear Jesus,

Thank You for loving me and for dying on the cross for me. I ask that You please forgive me of my sins and that You come into my heart. I need You and want to get to know You. Show me who You are. I want to love You. In Jesus' name. Amen.

It is that simple. Welcome to the family of God! May I encourage you to please get connected with a local church family that will help you learn more about what you have just done. If you do not know of one, please contact me and I will help you find one.

About the Author

Cheryl Stasinowsky is a speaker and writer of passion and transparency. Her desire is for others to see Jesus in everything they walk through; growing a new passion for His Word and its relevance for them. Please contact her to make arrangements for your future events, retreats, church services, meetings, and conferences. She would love to meet you!

www.hishiddentreasure.blogspot.com

psalm421@surewest.net

Connect with Cheryl on Facebook and twitter @histreasures too!

What others are saying:

"Cheryl Stasinowsky is a treasure. Cheryl is a special artist that paints her teachings in faith constructionism, and as such, she passionately extracts the blueprints from the foundation of the Word and then builds that foundation into the details of everyday practical life. Her books and teachings are a life guide, and her speaking appearances are personal. She opens herself to each person she is teaching, and lays out in honesty her own personal experiences of the presence of God within the joys and pains of everyday life."

More Titles by Cheryl Stasinowsky

His Hidden Treasures
ISBN: 978-0-6158979-9-8

There is an unknown treasure sitting on your night stand, bookshelf or coffee table. It is full of keys that will unlock your destiny, vision and purpose. They are yours for the taking. Join Cheryl on this journey as she uncovers valuable secrets found in the Bible. Through her own brokenness and surrender, the author will inspire you to embark on your own journey of searching for the timeless and endless treasures in the Word of God. As you dig deeper, each hidden treasure will leave you desperate for more of God's Word.

Deeper Relevance
ISBN: 978-0-6159069-9-7

Cheryl set out to write a daily encouraging word on her social networks, not realizing that her pursuit for a deeper understanding of God's Word would blossom into a full devotional. Grab your Bible, along with this book, and get ready to discover kingdom nuggets that will enrich your walk and relationship with Jesus. His Word truly sustains us every day!

More Titles by Cheryl Stasinowsky

Now Faith
ISBN: 978-0-615899-07-7

Now Faith is a face-to-face encounter with the men and women of Hebrews 11 who had the kind of faith that pleased God and moved mountains. Each chapter steps inside their lives, takes a look around, finds vital parts of the DNA of their faith, and then supplies a prayer for the impartation of that faith.

Now Faith in Spanish (Es Pues, La Fe)
ISBN: 978-0-615899-67-1

Es Pues, La Fe es un encuentro, cara a cara, con los hombres y mujeres de Hebreos 11 quienes tuvieron la fe que agradó a Dios y que movió montañas. Cada capítulo toma un paso adentro de sus vidas, echa un vistazo a su forma de ser, encuentra partes vitales del ADN de su fe, y después suple una oración para la impartición de esa fe.

More Titles by Cheryl Stasinowsky

Private Moments With God

ISBN: 978-0-6159103-7-6

Life as we individually know it ... Each of us has a past that is influencing how we see our present. We walk through our day with all of the pressures and demands of life with a past, in the present, and also with a hope for a future. I, too, journey this thing called life. Through it all, I have come to value to the highest degree the first moments of my early mornings when the house is quiet, it is still dark outside, my coffee is freshly brewed, my iPod is playing worship music in my ears, and I open the Word of God for my nourishment and encouragement for the day. These are those moments ...

Coming soon ...

GIVEN TO LOVE

GIVEN TO CHANGE

GIVEN TO NOT BE OFFENDED

GIVEN TO PRAYER

All of Cheryl's books are available in
eBook and print versions on Amazon and Barnes & Noble.

www.ingramcontent.com/pod-product-compliance
Lightning Source LLC
Chambersburg PA
CBHW071324040426
42444CB00009B/2074